LOST SOCK!

by Cynthia L. Copeland with Anya Lewis

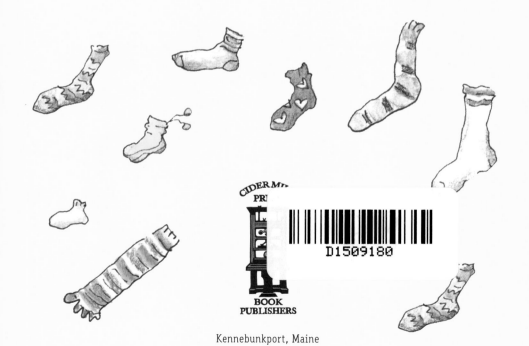

CIDER MILL
PRESS

BOOK
PUBLISHERS

Kennebunkport, Maine

Copyright © 2008 Cynthia L. Copeland and Anja Lewis

All rights reserved under the Pan-American and International Copyright Conventions.

No part of this book may be reproduced in whole or in part, scanned, photocopied, recorded, distributed in any printed or electronic form, or reproduced in any manner whatsoever, or by any information storage and retrieval system now known or hereafter invented, without express written permission of the publisher, except in the case of brief quotations embodied in critical articles and reviews.

The scanning, uploading, and distribution of this book via the Internet or via any other means without permission of the publisher is illegal and punishable by law. Please support authors' rights, and do not participate in or encourage piracy of copyrighted materials.

13-Digit ISBN: 978-1-60433-013-7
10-Digit ISBN: 1-60433-013-9

This book may be ordered by mail from the publisher. Please include $2.50 for postage and handling. Please support your local bookseller first!

Books published by Cider Mill Press Book Publishers are available at special discounts for bulk purchases in the United States by corporations, institutions, and other organizations. For more information, please contact the publisher.

Cider Mill Press Book Publishers
"Where good books are ready for press"
12 Port Farm Road
Kennebunkport, Maine 04046

Visit us on the web!
www.cidermillpress.com

Design by Jessica Disbrow
Illustrations by Cynthia L. Copeland

Printed in China

1 2 3 4 5 6 7 8 9 0
First Edition

FOR GAGA

cute little bob haircut

teeny but strong

always has something nice to say about everyone

is always smiling or laughing

wears very stylish clothes that she finds at bargain prices

is usually hugging a grandchild

TABLE OF CONTENTS

❊ INTRODUCTION ❊

THE MYSTERY OF THE
ODD SOCK

Socks come in pairs. You buy them, wear them, wash them, and dry them—together. So what happens? Why do you end up with so many unmatched socks in your drawer (some of which you've never seen before)?

❊ INTRODUCTION ❊

How can so many socks simply vanish? It's a more perplexing mystery than the Bermuda Triangle, black holes, and the Jimmy Hoffa disappearance rolled into one.

You can call these leftover socks single, solo, odd, lonely, stray, mateless . . . but you can't call them useless. Why, they can be re-invented in hundreds of ways with just a little effort and ingenuity. They can dress your daughter's Barbie doll, entertain your dog for hours, or clean your Venetian binds. They can be used in the garden or the garage, at the beach or in the barn.

Finding things to do with single socks is not only fun, it's also eco-friendly because it involves recycling. So that sock monkey on page 188 is, in reality, a major help to the environment.

We may never solve the mystery of the vanishing socks, but we can put the socks that do stick around to very good use. Read on . . .

—Cynthia L. Copeland with Anya Lewis

This pretty sock icon lets you know what projects are best for your most attractive socks.

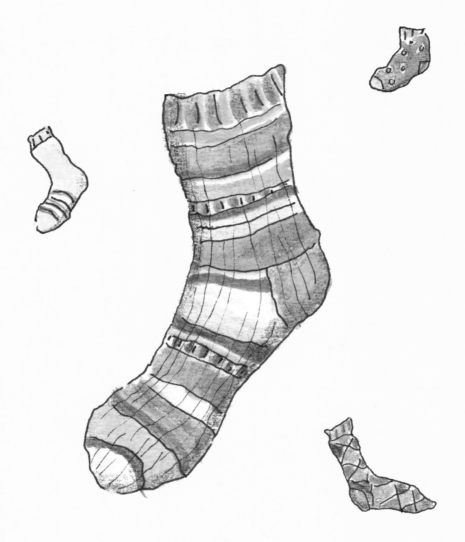

SOCKS FOR PETS

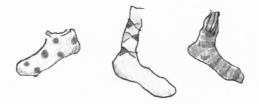

Whether you have a hamster or a horse, you can find all sorts of ways to use single socks to help your animal friends. An added bonus: animals are not embarrassed to wear clothes or play with toys made of odd socks, even in front of their friends.

FUN SOCKS FOR DOGS

○ Tie a knot or two in a sock for an instant dog toy, or tie three or four socks together if you have a big, active dog.

○ Make a chew toy for your dog by putting a bone or some treats inside a sock; he'll have fun (or go insane) trying to get at the treat.

● On a hot day, put a few ice cubes in a sock, knot the top, and give it to your dog for a cool outdoor treat.

● Tie old dog toys together with socks. Your dog will think it's a new toy.

NOTE: This doesn't work with kids. If you tie their old toys together with socks, they will not believe it's a new toy.

● Buy a replacement squeaker for pet toys. Wrap it in several pairs of socks, and then put it into another sock. Tie the end tightly. It will be just as sturdy as a toy you'd buy in the pet store.

● Put a few pebbles into an empty plastic water bottle. Slide the bottle, cap side up, into a sock and tie the end. Your pup will have the pleasure of crunching the plastic and shaking it to rattle the pebbles.

○ Thread a large plastic bottle cap, toilet paper tube, yogurt container, or anything you think will work through a long tube sock and tie it at both ends for a great dog toy.

○ Put a tennis ball in the toe of a sock, tie a knot, put in another ball, and tie another knot. Toss it to your puppy and watch her have fun!

● Stuff stiff paper (that will make a delightfully crinkly noise) into a sock, tie it at the end, and toss it to your dog.

● If you are sewing a toy for your dog, stuff it with odd socks.

are throx the answer?

A product called Throx bills itself as the cure for missing socks. Throx socks come in threes, so that when one disappears, a pair remains. (The idea has potential, although threesomes rarely end well. Somebody always feels left out.) Visit www.throx.com for more information.

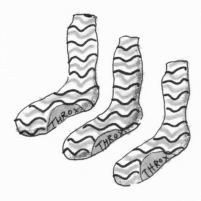

FUN SOCKS
FOR OTHER PETS

○ Cut the toes off of several socks, then sew them together to make a "tunnel" for your caged pets like mice and gerbils.

○ Tie a few socks together to make a tug for your ferret. To make a strong tug for a big dog, cut socks into strips, braid them, and then braid three of those together. Tie tightly at both ends.

○ For a stimulating cat toy, pack a sock with catnip (and with another sock or two), then sew or tie it closed. For extra fun, pull some threads loose for the cat to play with.

○ Stuff a small sock with another small sock, tie a knot in it, and attach it to a piece of string or an old shoelace. Pull it around the house and your cat will be in hot pursuit. (You can also attach it from a piece of furniture or a doorjamb so that it dangles down and the cat can bat at it.)

○ For hamsters, gerbils, or rats, put treats into a sock, knot it, and then tie it to the roof of the cage with a piece of string so that it dangles within reach. Your little critters will enjoy gnawing at the sock to get at the goodies inside.

● Sew a large bell onto the toe of a sock, the turn the sock inside out to make a ball. Pull another sock on top so that your cat can't get to the bell.

 # USEFUL
SOCKS FOR PETS

 Put socks on your pet's paws to keep them warm in the winter.

○ After cutting off the toe, use a sock as a bandage for a dog or a larger animal, such as a horse.

○ Use a sock in a fish tank as a filter media. Put the carbon or ammonia remover chips in a sock, then in the filter. You'll save money on the sleeves you usually buy at the pet store.

○ Pull on mismatched socks over your hands when you are giving your pet a bath.

○ Tear socks into strips and use as bedding for bunnies, gerbils, or other caged pets.

○ When you are heading outside with your dog, put his treats in a sock before sticking them in your pocket. Whoever does the laundry will thank you.

○ On chilly days, fill a sock with rice and tie the end. Warm (do not heat) in the microwave and then put it in the cage with your little rodent friends so that they can snuggle up and stay toasty.

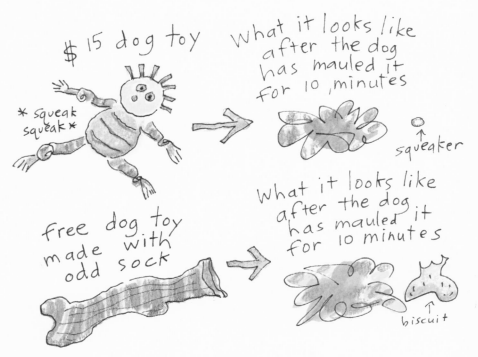

$15 dog toy

* squeak squeak *

What it looks like after the dog has mauled it for 10 minutes

↑ squeaker

free dog toy made with odd sock

What it looks like after the dog has mauled it for 10 minutes

↑ biscuit

my sock story

"Years ago, the lint filter in our dryer went missing (long story . . .). Anyway, before we realized it and replaced it, socks (and other small items) shot out the dryer vent into the front yard. I'm sure the neighbors went crazy during that time trying to figure out why we would all come outside and search through the grass, shouting with delight when we found an odd sock or pair of underpants."

-Anna-Louise

YOUR SINGLE SOCKS CAN HELP HOMELESS CATS!

The mission of Operation Happy Sock, founded by Martha Powers of Fairfax, Virginia, is to make catnip treats for cats living in shelters. Volunteers collect unwanted socks, fill them with catnip and polyester fiberfill, and then deliver them to animal shelters. If you would like a free information kit to start an Operation Happy Sock group in your area, visit Martha's Web site at www.operationhappysock.com.

 # sock tip #1

Safety pin your socks together
before putting them in the hamper.

SOCK ALERT

Some dogs eat socks (as well as other things not normally considered food). This is a condition known as pica and may be a result of anxiety, a desire for attention, or an attempt to get nutrients the dog isn't getting from his diet. Unfortunately, this habit can be very dangerous and lead to serious health issues. Although it does reduce the number of odd socks you have (and cut down on your dog food bill), allowing your pet to eat them is not advisable.

missing

MISSING

AGE OF SOCK AT DISAPPEARANCE:
8 months

ETHNIC BACKGROUND:
Made in China

COLOR: White, with stripes

DISTINGUISHING MARKS:
Nike-like logo on left side

LAST SEEN WITH: Sock of same
description in upstairs hamper

IF SPOTTED, CONTACT: Charlie

SOCKS OVER SHOES

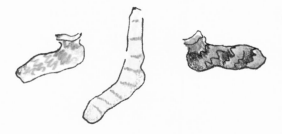

Try a little role reversal for your shoes and socks. Let the socks be the ones on top. It's a bit of an ego boost for the sock community, and in the following instances, it makes a lot of sense.

○ Pull big socks over your shoes if you have to walk on an icy path or driveway. They make the going a bit less slippery.

○ When packing your suitcase, protect your clothes from dirty shoes by sliding your shoes into odd socks.

○ If you are painting and want to keep your shoes from getting splattered, slip single socks over them.

○ In the laundry room, keep old socks around for times when you wash comforters or pillows. Put a sock over a clean shoe in the dryer—the shoe bounces around and keeps the stuffing evenly dispersed. (You can also use a tennis ball or fluffing rings inside a sock for the same purpose.)

○ If you get tired of tying and untying your little tykes' shoes as they go in and out of the house, have them pull old socks on over their shoes as they come in.

the seven most common missing sock theories

○ The sock monster that lives in the dryer has eaten them. (The lint trap contains the digested remains of the socks.)

○ Socks are cannibals. Corresponding theory #1: Male socks eat their young; #2: Female socks eat the males after mating.

○ Socks get tired of their mates and run away. Like people, they crave variety.

- Socks reproduce in the dryer; the single socks you find after doing laundry are actually offspring.

- The spinning action of the dryer creates a kind of time warp deal in which socks are sucked into a parallel universe. (Note to Steven Spielberg: Great movie theme or what?)

- Socks are really the pupa stage of plastic bags, so as the socks morph, you'll notice a shortage of socks and an over-abundance of plastic bags.

- According to the Sock String Theory, socks are made up of teeny tiny threads that vibrate at a frequency that sends certain socks into a previously unknown 26th dimension.

SOCKS FOR TOTS

Be sure to use these ideas while your kids are little because it doesn't take long before they develop firm ideas about what they will and will not wear. One day, they're perfectly content wearing mittens made from odd socks, and the next day they want to look "normal." Go figure.

TEENY TOTS!

⊙ If you have a crawling baby, cut off the toes of two adult socks and pull the socks over the baby's knees for some extra padding.

⊙ Cut the toe off of an odd sock and slip it over the buckle piece of a baby's car seat. The sock will provide a bit of extra padding between the baby's legs.

⊙ Cut off the feet of long socks so toddlers can slip the remaining "tube" on under their pants for leg warmers on cold days.

 Roll an odd sock into a ball for a safe baby toy.

◉ Unless your baby is on her way to Sears Portrait Studio, put oversized odd socks on her, then pull her pants on over the socks. They will stay on much better than booties or little shoes (even though they are not as cute to look at).

 Pull a single sock over a baby bottle so that it's easier to grip.

○ Sew a small rattle onto an old sock and slip the sock on an infant's foot. As she moves, she will shake the rattle. Soon, she'll associate moving her foot with the noise.

rattle
rattle

sock tip #2

Buy all white socks, all the time.

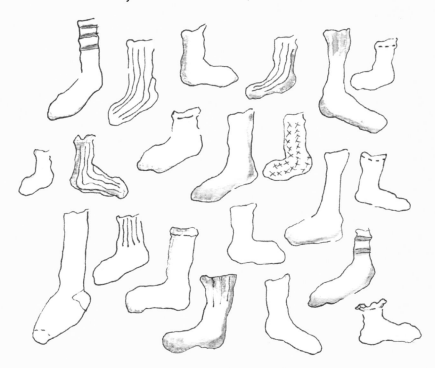

BIGGER TOTS!

● Fill a sock with baby powder, tie the end, and let kids dust themselves after a bath. The powder will seep through the sock, making it much neater than allowing them to shake the baby powder container.

If you are having an outdoor party for one of your kids, anchor the balloon bouquet to a sock filled with sand or stones (and tied at the top).

● Kids can put old socks over their hands when cleaning their bikes so that they can get to all of the hard-to-reach spots.

⊙ With a quick face drawn on by a laundry marker, socks can become bath puppets for kids. (And, with a little liquid soap, they make excellent washcloths for kids learning to wash themselves up.)

⊙ Fill socks with flour, tie them at the ends, and direct your kids to the driveway where they can pound out a fun design in flour.

○ Odd socks can be used to hold beads, marbles, small toys, or game pieces. Tie a loose knot and toss it in the toy box.

○ Cut off the foot of two long socks and sew them to mittens. They'll tuck under sleeves and stay on better than mittens alone.

○   To wash little plastic toys like Legos, put them in a sock, tie the end, and give it to the kids in the bathtub. They can squirt the sock with liquid soap and smoosh it around to get the toys clean.

○   Make a slit in the bottom of an old sock and pull it over a child's ice skate to help keep her foot warmer. Use a shoelace to tie the sock in place.

○   If someone is expecting a visit from the tooth fairy, he should put his tooth in a sock and leave the sock under his pillow, with just the end sticking out. It won't affect his sleep when the tooth fairy visits because she won't have to fish around under his pillow for 10 minutes in search of the tooth.

When children are counting down the days until an important occasion, clip a series of odd socks (one for each day) to a long piece of ribbon and hang it in the child's room. Fill each sock with a message, a wish, small treat, or anything appropriate to the upcoming occasion. The child can take down one sock each day until the big event.

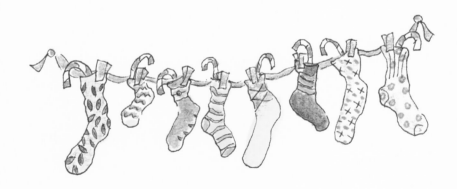

○ Use long socks under mittens to add an extra layer of warmth. (You can cut a small hole in the sock for your thumb.)

○ When your kids are headed out to play in the stream or the swamp (or any place with the potential for getting dirty), put them in a pair of unmatched socks. Save the matching socks for school, and save yourself some time and energy by tossing the dirty odd socks in the trash when the kids are done playing.

# WHILE
YOU'RE ON THE PHONE

If you need to make a phone call (but don't want little voices interrupting you), plan ahead. Hide 20 odd socks all over the house (with just the toes sticking out) and hide one pair that matches. Tell your kids that while you are busy, they can try to find all the socks, and whoever finds the one matching pair gets a prize. (If you're feeling thrifty, a head rub; if you're feeling generous, a pony.)

 # sad sock truths

○ The mold-colored socks that Auntie Betty passed along to your husband after Uncle Charlie died will never get lost, but one of the fluffy socks you splurged on yesterday will vanish within 2 weeks.

○ If you turn a solo sock into a sock puppet, its mate will turn up within 24 hours.

○ Socks that have holes in them always match up with socks with no holes, leaving you in a quandary.

RAINY DAYS
ODD SOCKS,
& BORED KIDS: 5 IDEAS

○ Challenge little kids to organize unmatched socks by color, size, or pattern.

○ Lay out several white socks and ask the kids to tell you all the ways they are different.

● Pay them 25 cents a pair to match the socks. (You are the ultimate judge of whether they have found a match or are stretching it.)

● Make it a competition: Dump all of the mismatched socks on the floor, set a timer for 5 minutes, and see who can find the most pairs.

● Put a small item in an odd sock and tie the open end. See how long it takes your child to guess what the item is by feeling it through the sock.

happy sock truths

○ Without a basket of odd socks to try to match up, you would have no excuse to watch the entire *Sylvester Stallone: E! True Hollywood Story.*

○ Often the most profound, life-altering realizations come to you while you are doing something mindless, like matching socks.

○ You test your creativity and flexibility by joining pairs of socks that did not start out together.

SOCK-MATCHING INCENTIVE PROGRAM

No matter how much you plead, kids rarely make the effort to pair up their socks before putting them in the hamper. They need a carefully crafted incentive program designed by someone who understands what really motivates kids. With the Sock Exchange Program, children can swap a certain number of pairs of dirty, balled-up socks for things they really want.

Here is a chart showing the exchange values:

NUMBER OF PAIRS	EXCHANGE VALUE
1	Child is permitted to sing along with songs on the car radio for one day, despite the fact that it drives siblings crazy.
2	Child can drink from the prized dragon cup (make appropriate substitution) and can choose to have his sibling drink from the undesirable plastic Elmo cup (again, substitute to apply to your family).
3	Child is permitted to sit in the front seat of the car for the entire day, even if another child "calls" it; this includes radio station selection privileges as well as heat/AC control.
4	Child may delegate one chore to a sibling, including, but not limited to, dog walking, table clearing, bed making, or garbage take-out duty.
5	On the next occasion, child may choose the babysitter, restaurant, movie, board game, or bedtime story.

SOCKS WITH A MESSAGE

Your socks speak a universal language—of lust, territorialism, and danger. (You had no idea, did you?)

sock brain teaser

If the average life of a pair of socks is 5 weeks (after which only one will remain) and your child requires 12 pairs of socks at any given time, how many pairs of socks will you need to purchase each year in order to maintain the appropriate pair number? (Factor in the knowledge that if you have a girl, she will likely go through at least a 1-month phase where she will prefer wearing mismatched socks.)

Answer: Factoring in two sleepovers per month (which will yield 7 abandoned socks) and two trips to the school's Lost and Found (5 socks recovered per trip), the answer is six. Ish. Six-ish.

sock tip #3

Use rubber bands to keep a pair together.

PRETTY SOCKS

Let's face it: pretty socks are harder to throw away than ugly ones. People might not admit it, but we all know it's true. So it's even more important for us to find ways to use our pretty single stockings. In fact, watch for this icon throughout the book for other ways to use especially attractive socks.

● If you are hosting a baby shower luncheon or throwing a first birthday party, use cute little solo socks to hold silverware at each place setting.

● Pull a pretty sock over a small flower pot to add some color.

● Slip a colorful sock over a plain glass jar and fill it with candy or potpourri.

 # sock tip #4

Forget about socks altogether.
Wear sandals, then switch to bare feet in boots.

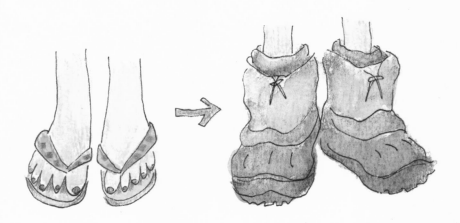

LOTS OF SOCKS

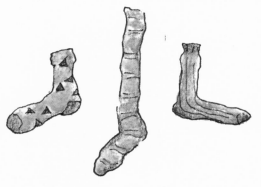

If you have a sock mountain rather than a sock pile, you'll need to use your odd socks by the dozens, not just one by one. Here are some good ideas for the owner of multiple mismatched socks.

 Make a (warm, washable, though not particularly attractive) sock blanket. (Instructions are on page 76.)

 Make three different kinds of rugs out of odd socks. (Instructions begin on page 80.)

crafty sock tip

If you are making something out of white socks that needs a little pizzazz, use Rit dye to add color. You can buy the dye at most department stores, or visit www.ritdye.com.

○ Stuff a pet's bed or kid's lounging pillow with odd socks.

○ Make a sock jump rope. Tie approximately 15 long socks together for a functional jump rope or, for something a little fancier, cut off the toes and sew a tube out of a variety of colored socks.

sock tip #5

Wash pairs of socks in a lingerie bag.

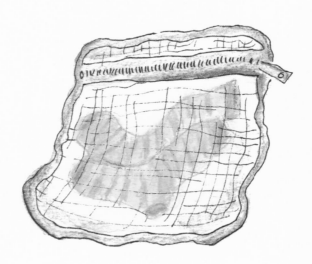

THE SOCK LADY

The Sock Lady of South Strafford, Vermont, uses old socks to make beautiful, one-of-a-kind, woven rugs. Check out her work at www.socklady.com.

the Sock Lady lives here

single socks historical fact

Wearing mismatched socks dates from the Middle Ages, when it was fashionable to wear two different colored stockings. Paintings from this era show royalty posing with mismatched socks, often with each leg being an entirely different color. So, as it turns out, your little princess is not being rebellious when she wears one purple sock and one black sock; she's just going back to her roots.

HOW TO MAKE AN ODD-SOCK BLANKET

Using socks of the same approximate length and width, lay them out side by side with the first one toe up, the next one toe down, and so on. The heels should all be on the underside of the "blanket." (This makes one row of socks. You can make as many rows as you like, depending how big you want the blanket to be.) Use a darning needle and thread to stitch the socks together, beginning inside the toe of a sock to hide the knot in the thread.

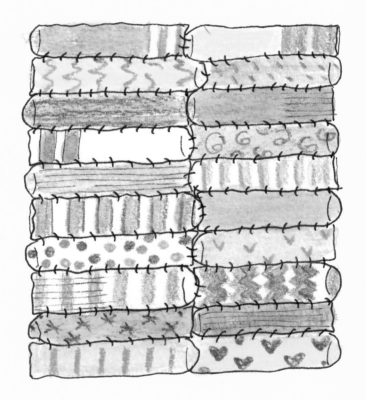

products that promise to keep socks together

○ CYCLOPS SOCK CLIPS

Available at www.cyclopssockclip.com, these plastic clips keep your socks together from the hamper all the way to the laundry basket. Available in multipacks of five colors. The company promises to "keep an eye on your socks."

⦿ SOCKS LOCKS

At just $3 for a pack of 32, you'll have all your sock pairs mated for life. They're available in nine colors, so even if you're the Waltons or the Von Trapps, each family member has his or her own color. Check out www.sock-locks.com.

⦿ SOCK PRO SOCK HOLDERS

This product, created by a frustrated father of three, is available in packages of 20 for $4.99. So far, he's sold a million holders to other frustrated fathers (and mothers). See www.sockpro.com or call 1-800-SOCKpro for more information.

3 WAYS TO MAKE
SOCK RUGS

○ Make a round sock rug using ankle socks. Beginning with the smallest one, lay the socks on their sides (with the heels all facing the same way) in a spiral pattern. Tuck the toe of one sock into the top opening of the next and sew them together with a darning needle and thread. As you continue, you will create a long, spiral-shaped tube of socks. When you have used up all of your socks, begin at the center of the spiral and stitch the socks together to form a tight, circular rug.

○ To make a shag sock rug, you'll need to buy a piece of rug canvas, which is stiff and has a loose weave with large holes. (A piece of burlap works also, but it must be stretched over a wooden frame.) Cut your odd socks into strips of about 1 inch by 3 or 4 inches. With the underside of the rug facing up, push one end of a sock strip through the canvas with a knitting needle. About a $1/4$ inch over, push the other end through. Flip the rug over and pull on the two rag ends until they are tight and even. Continue "prodding" (the rug-maker's term) until you've created a nice, shaggy pile and the canvas is no longer visible on the rug's right side.

○ For a rectangular braided sock rug, cut many colorful socks into strips 2 or 3 inches wide (with a diagonal cut on the end). Sew the socks together to make three strips of about 8 or 9 feet each. Before you begin braiding, pin together the three ends of the sock "tubes" and attach that end to something stable. Braid the sock tubes until you achieve the desired length. Pin the end to keep it from unraveling, cut the sock tubes, and begin another braid. When you have braided enough pieces for a rug, lay them out next to each other. Stitch the ends, making sure the rug will be even. Then sew the braids together with carpet thread.

 # single socks in literature

Single socks have not been overlooked as a literary theme. The self-published *Sid the Sock Eating Monster* by Awen Little tells a story that is essentially explained by its title. Also, a series of children's books called *The Oddies* by Grant Slatter follows the wacky adventures of a gang of single socks. (I smell a Pulitzer!)

SOCKS IN THE GARDEN

Gardeners come up with all sorts of clever ideas to help them in their hobby, using everything from dryer lint to coat hangers. So it's no surprise that these practical folks have come up with ways to put odd socks to good use outside.

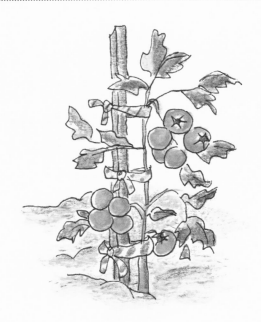

○ Cut socks into long strips to use to tie tomato plants or flowers to support posts. Because they're somewhat stretchy, socks are better than twine or rope.

○ If socks are 100 percent cotton, soak them in water and bury them under thirsty plants in your garden for continuous watering.

⊙ Put a bar of soap into a long sock and tie a knot near the soap. Tie the open end of the sock to an outdoor faucet or a water jug. You can wash your hands without going into the house.

⊙ Fill odd socks with blood meal and place them around your garden to help keep rabbits and deer away.

⊙ Put a sock over your hand to weed so that your hands stay clean. Then just throw the dirty sock away!

 If you are digging up a plant to give a friend, use a sock to hold it, just like trees and shrubs at the nursery have their roots wrapped in burlap bags.

● Store plant bulbs in odd socks.

Note: I made up the stuff about dryer lint and coat hangers so don't waste your time searching the Internet for ways to use them in the garden. I just wanted to make the point that gardeners are a resourceful bunch and know how to put seemingly useless things to good use.

sock events

Every spring since the mid-1980s, sailors in Annapolis, Maryland, have taken part in the ceremonial Burning of the Socks, an event that celebrates the fact that it will soon be warm enough to wear boat shoes without socks. The event draws more than a hundred boat owners and boatyard workers who, anxious for warm weather to arrive, delight in tossing their unwanted socks on the blaze. (A great way to unload that bag of single socks, once and for all!)

SOCKS AT PLAY

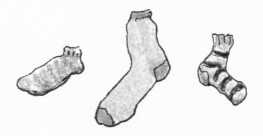

Odd socks are fun by nature, so play comes naturally to them. Whether you're making a toy with an extra sock or using it to help you carry your sports equipment, you'll be happy you've accumulated a few mismatched socks.

Put a tennis ball in the toe end of a sock, tie a knot near the opening, and grab the knot to toss it like a Foxtail Softie (a popular toy that features a ball with a ribbon tail attached to it).

○ Pull socks over the end of hockey sticks so that you can play indoors without scratching the floor.

- Roll odd socks into balls and play games.

- Cut the top 2 inches off two odd socks to use as sweat bands.

- Make a footbag (otherwise known as a Hacky Sack) or a beanbag by filling the toe end of a sock with dried rice, sewing it closed, and cutting off the excess sock.

O Use socks for a kinder, gentler game of paintball. Fill dozens of odd nylon socks or knee highs with flour and tie the open end. Give them to kids (outside) to throw at one another for a certain period of time. When time's up, players count how often they've been tagged (or marked with flour). Once a winner has been declared, the "paint balls" can be collected and used again.

O Slide a toe-less sock over skis to hold them together.

Turn an odd sock into a sock puppet.

A VERY SHORT PLAY, STARRING YOUR SOCK PUPPETS

THE WIDE-MOUTH FROG

○ CAST

The Wide-Mouth Frog sock puppet and four to six other assorted sock puppets

○ SCRIPT

Frog (who speaks with his mouth WIDE open) approaches each of the sock puppets in turn, saying: "Hi! I'm a wide-mouth frog! I like to eat spiders and flies! Who are you and what do you like to eat?"

Each puppet answers appropriately until the last one. The final sock puppet tells the frog who he is and then he says, "I like to eat wide-mouth frogs."

Frog (pursing his lips together so that they barely move): "Oh. Well, I haven't seen any of those around."

○   Use odd socks as skate guards. Tie a sock at the opening and make a slit down the side. Pull it over your skates to protect the blade when you are transporting your skates to the rink.

○   Cut the top few inches off an old sock and use it to hold your pant leg so that it won't get caught in the chain when you are riding your bike.

If you're playing a sport, slip a sock onto your water bottle. The water will stay colder, and the sock will absorb any sweat from your hands.

- Use socks as markers for outside games (such as first base, home plate, and so on) . . . if they get left behind, no big deal.

- Cut the toe off of a sock and slide it onto your arm or leg to hold a knee or elbow pad in place.

- For an impromptu game of Pin-the-Tail on the Donkey, you can cut a sock up two sides to make a long strip that can be used as a blindfold. (I hope I'm not giving kidnappers any ideas here . . . That's why it's under the "Play" section of the book rather than the "Crime" section.)

SOCK-TAIL TAG

One player tucks a sock into the back of his waistband and begins to run. Those chasing him must grab the sock and pull it free. Whoever does that becomes "it," the one with the sock tail.

enter at your own risk

SOCK-BALL BOWLING

Here's a great indoor game for a rainy day. Find several cardboard toilet paper and paper towel tubes. Stuff each with a sock and set them up like bowling pins. Stand as far away as you can and throw a sock ball toward them, trying to knock them all down. Keep score as you would for a bowling game.

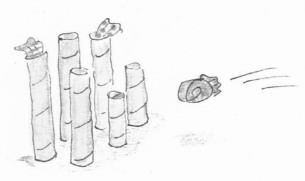

odd socks and true crime stories

○ A newspaper article reported that an area burglar wore the homeowner's socks over his hands so he wouldn't leave prints.

○ A New Mexico woman escaped from leg irons because she was wearing six socks on each foot and was able to wiggle free, only to be caught within a matter of seconds by an officer standing nearby.

○ A gang of thieves in England stole 50 boxes of odd socks that were headed for a Woolworths store as part of a promotion for a children's book series called *The Oddies*.

SOCK-BALL PLAY

⊙ Set a row of large plastic cups on the floor and stand back several feet. Try to throw your sock ball into one of the cups without knocking it over. The cup closest to you is worth one point, with a point added as the cups get farther away.

⊙ Squeeze a sock ball between your knees and have your friends do the same. See who can run the fastest without dropping the sock ball. Next, try running as you hold a sock ball balanced on top of an empty paper towel tube.

◎   For a game of indoor baseball, roll up a newspaper or magazine (or find a sturdy cardboard wrapping paper tube) to make a bat and use a rolled up sock for a ball. (You won't want to play this game in the room where your mother's antique tea cup collection is displayed.)

◎   Juggle three sock balls.

SEXY SOCKS

This section is rated R, so skip it unless you have a risqué side to you.

● Stuff socks in your bra for instant enhancement.

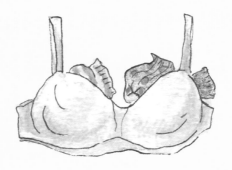

● Guys can stuff socks in their pants to encourage extra attention from the ladies.

sock haiku

socks that stray:

looking for a sole mate,

not a perfect match

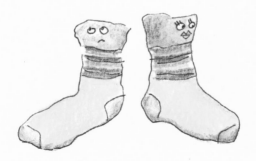

THRIFTY
SOCKS

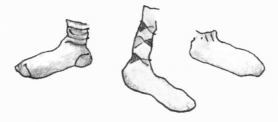

Some of these ideas require a bit of time and effort on your part, and some simply require that you don't care what others think about you (as with the suggestion for golfers). But if you're frugal, you won't mind the strange stares or extra effort these things involve. You'll be downright giddy about all of the money you've saved by using the odd socks that spendthrifts would merely have thrown away.

🧦 Fill a sock with small stones for a door stop.

🔵 Make a sock mop. Cut several socks in half, lay them flat, and attach an old wooden mop clip; or secure the sock strips to a broom handle using a rubber band.

🧦 Starting at the open end, cut across the sock every inch or so to make loops that can be used as hair ties. These "scrunchies" can go swimming, to camp, or anywhere an expensive hair tie shouldn't go.

- Fill and decorate a sock for a stuffed animal or a doll.

- Use odd sock as golf club covers (but only after you've been accepted as a member of the country club).

 Single socks can be used as Christmas stockings. Not only will you save money on the stockings themselves, but they're not as large as the store-bought stockings, so Santa will save some money filling them. (An added bonus: the kids will have fun decorating them.)

● Remove the toes of two socks and turn what's left into cuffs for a sweatshirt or jacket whose sleeves have gotten too short.

 Instead of a coaster, slip the toe end of an odd sock over the bottom of a drinking glass to avoid leaving rings.

 Use the toe part of a single sock to cover a pony tail and create a bun.

● Cut off the toes of two odd socks, make thumb holes, and you have a pair of fingerless gloves!

 Cut off the toes of odd socks to create "tubes" and then sew the socks together to create an extended tube. You can stuff the sock tube with beans or rice (or even other socks!), sew the ends, and use it to stop window or door drafts.

single socks and your dating personality: a quiz

*How you respond to your orphan socks
says a lot about your love life.*

○   You keep your bags of mismatched socks for years,
even taking them with you when you move, always making
a place for them in the laundry room.*

*This is especially serious if you also save single socks that
have holes in them.

You are never the one who breaks off a relationship. Instead, you hang on forever, even to the real losers, desperately hoping that the situation will change and he'll stop leaving pizza crusts in bed or blowing his nose in whatever's on top in the hamper.

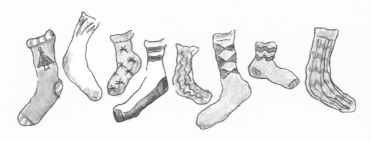

○ You see every single sock as a potential craft project.

You analyze your dates in terms of what you can do to make them cuter, more useful, and more appealing. You imagine what he'd look like with a little more stuffing, a few nips and tucks, even an entirely new job!

○ You donate your bag of solo socks to Goodwill.

After you break off a relationship, you fix the guy up with one of your friends, as if you were doing a good deed. Everybody knows, however, that giving away your cast-offs isn't really giving. We can all find our own pathetic losers, thank you very much.

○ You turn them into rags within a reasonable period of time.

You give a relationship about 6 months, and if it doesn't seem to gel in that period of time, you break up with him, assuring him that he will find someone else who really wants him and who will put him to good use.

SOCKS IN YOUR CAR

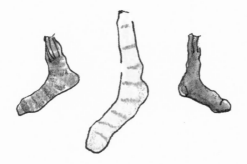

There are all sorts of reasons to keep a bag of single socks in your car, along with a flashlight, flares, goldfish crackers for nibbling, the book on CD you can't follow because the reader has a weird accent, and maps of places you drove to one time and will never visit again.

 Use an odd sock as a gear shift cover so that the knob is not uncomfortably hot in the summer or cold in the winter.

⊙ If it snows while you're out, you can pull socks over your hands and clear the windshield.

⊙ Do a quick clean of the dashboard area with a sock over your hand if you suddenly discover you'll be driving your boss home from work.

○ Apply wax to your car with a solo sock over your hand.

○ If you need to change a flat tire, you can put socks over your hands so they will stay clean.

○ If you are too small for your seat belt, cut the toe off of a single sock and slide the remaining portion of the sock up the seat belt so that it pulls the upper part of the belt down for a more comfortable fit.

⊙ If you tend to hit your head on your roof rack, slip a sock on any piece that juts out and secure it with a rubber band.

⊙ Use a long, stretchy trouser sock to tie the trunk down if you have bought an oversized item.

○ Clean the inside of a foggy windshield with a sock over your hand.

○ When you are checking to see if you have enough oil, wipe the dip stick on an old sock.

○ Use a solo sock to protect a CD that's lost its cover.

sock pie chart

Types of Socks Left Single

- white socks
- black socks
- blue socks
- socks no one has ever seen before
- baby socks (even though no one in the family is under age 20)
- peds with the word "cheer" on them (even though no one in the family is a cheerleader)
- Socks that might have a mate but are so misshapen that it's impossible to tell

sock brain teaser

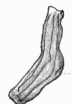

You close your eyes and reach into your sock drawer, knowing you have twelve white socks and twelve blue socks. What is the minimum number of socks you have to take out of the drawer to be certain you'll have a pair that matches, realizing that seven of the white socks and four of the blue socks have weird patterns that don't match any of the others?

Answer: The answer is pi because it sounds yummy. If "pi" doesn't produce a pair, that's a sign that you should just wear sandals.

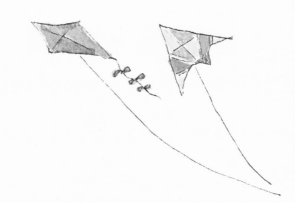

SOCKS AT THE BEACH

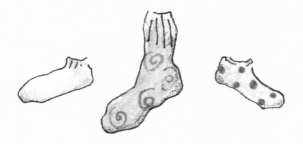

Towels, sunscreen, a beach ball . . . and odd socks. You might not think to add them to your list, but once you've spent a day at the beach with socks, you'll never take another seaside trip without them.

⊙ Use odd socks for collecting pretty shells, stones, or sea glass.

⊙ Fill single socks with rocks to hold down the corners of a blanket if it's a blustery beach day.

⊙ Fill a tube sock with sand to use as a "bat" and take swings at a sock rolled into a ball.

○ Fill odd socks with sand, tie them at the top, and play "socker" golf: Dig a hole in the sand and give each player a sand-filled sock (or a rolled-up sock, which means the wind might play a role in the game's outcome). Start far away from the hole, toss the sock toward the hole, then take turns trying to throw it into the hole from wherever it lands. As in golf, the lowest score wins.

● Roll odd socks into balls and toss them into the wind for others to try to catch.

● If you will be bobbing in a boat, a sock pulled over the bottom of a soda can or bottle can prevent your drink from sliding into the water when things get choppy.

● Find a volleyball net (or tie a towel between two beach chairs) and play games with a sand-filled sock similar to those you would play with a footbag.

 fighting for odd socks

In the summer of 2007, middle school students in Napa, California, went to court and fought for the right to wear socks with patterns, cartoon characters, or symbols, despite the school's contention that its strict uniform rules applied to socks. With the backing of the American Civil Liberties Union, the students won. A victory for funky socks everywhere!

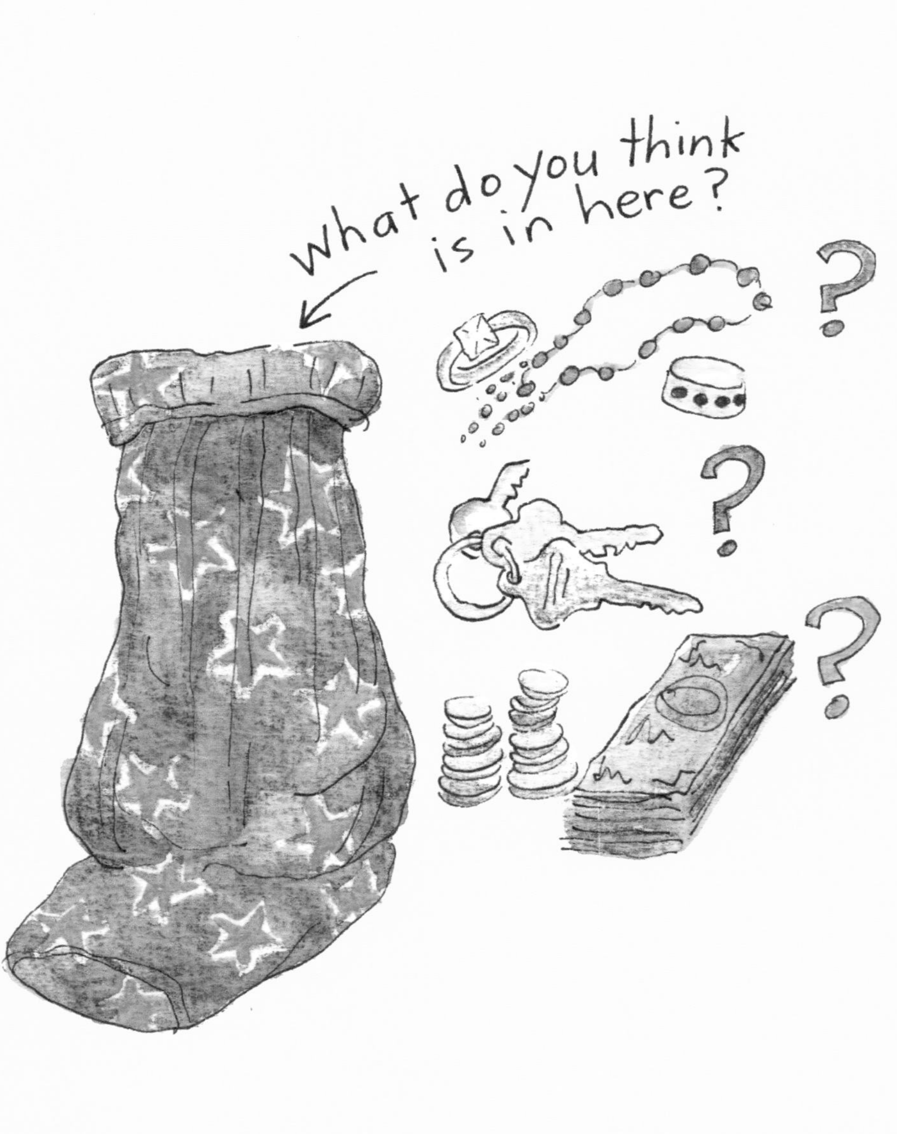
What do you think is in here?

SNEAKY SOCKS

If you didn't think socks could be sneaky, take a peek at these ideas.

- Hide jewelry or other valuables inside a single sock, then tuck it in your sock drawer or into your suitcase if you're traveling.

 Use a sock to discreetly hold feminine products in a school backpack or gym locker.

- At the pool or beach, tuck your wallet and car keys into a sock before you take a dip.

○ At the office, slip candy, change, or anything you might want to horde into a sock, ball up the sock, and toss it into your bottom desk drawer.

○ If you've bought small Christmas or birthday gifts— jewelry, an iPod, perfume—tuck them into odd socks to keep them from being discovered.

missing socks: the scene of the crime

When does the system break down, we wonder? Can we identify the exact moment when a sock gets separated from its mate? If so, perhaps we can prevent the epidemic of single socks.

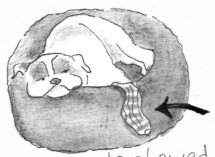

sock gets chewed on and ends up in dog's bed

sock gets left at summer camp

sock gets left
in boot

sock gets stuck to towel
when coming out of dryer

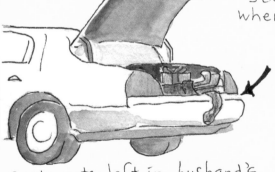

sock gets left in husband's
trunk along with golf shoes,
golf clubs, energy bars he bought
but doesn't like, Christmas gift
he keeps forgetting to drop off with
the neighbors and 3 baseball hats

sock falls behind
hamper in bathroom

DOLLS & SOCKS

Your kids will have more fun making clothes and accessories for their dolls than they would buying them. Keep a craft box filled with beads, glue, glitter, pom-poms, fabric trim, and buttons that they can use to enhance their original creations.

Frilly socks can be turned into Barbie® doll clothes by cutting off the toe and making arm holes.

A baby sock makes a cute doll's hat.

- Solo socks can become comfy sleeping bags for dolls.

- Strips of knee highs turn into doll belts and hair ties.

○ Keep doll shoes, combs, and other tiny accessories from getting lost by storing them in a sock.

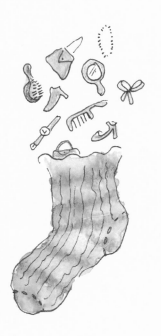 Cut off the toe of a pretty sock, then cut the remaining sock up the side to make a doll's rug or blanket.

famous sock, r-rated

Ed the Sock was created in the 1990s by Steve Joel Kerzner, then program director for an Ontario community television station. In an attempt to attract viewers, Steve created a sock puppet with bottle cap eyes and a half-smoked cigar who was free to crack inappropriate jokes and make wise comments. Ed went on to co-host City TV's "Ed's Night Party," a racy adult talk show, with a buxom red-head named Liana K (Steve's wife), and was a frequent host on MuchMusic. A bit of Ed trivia: he's 20 percent nylon and 80 percent cotton.

SOCKS IN A PINCH

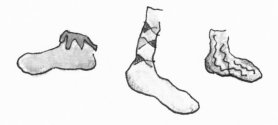

You never know when you might be out of coffee filters or getting ready to sneeze with no tissues in sight. Socks can come in handy at times like these. Although they might not be ideal ways to use your odd socks, it's better to have a sock nearby than nothing at all.

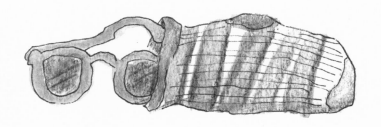

Slip glasses into a sock to keep them from getting scratched.

○ Use a sock as a handkerchief if you are desperate.

○ Use a sock to tie a gate closed if you have no chain or rope available.

○ In a real emergency, feminine, um, needs can be temporarily managed with an odd sock.

○ Use a sock to hold the quarters you are bringing to the Laundromat.

If you need something to hold your pencils, you can use a sock.

• A sock will sop up a messy spill, like motor oil in the garage or ketchup on the deck. Then just toss it in the garbage.

• A sock can keep screws, nails, nuts, and bolts from getting lost in the garage.

- Use a sock to tie two pieces of a fishing rod together to make it easier to carry.

- By filling it with rocks or sand, a sock becomes an instant anchor.

- In a real emergency, use a sock as a coffee filter.

- Stray socks can be used as whiteboard erasers.

famous sock, g-rated

The spirited yet vulnerable Lamb Chop, a sock puppet sheep, was created by comedian and ventriloquist Shari Lewis in 1957. Lewis and Lamb Chop initially appeared on a local morning show that aired in New York; then, in the 1960s, the pair starred in a musical-comedy show on network television. *Lamb Chop's Play-Along* debuted on PBS in 1992 and went on to win numerous Emmys. Lamb Chop's sidekicks, also made from socks, were Hush Puppy and Charlie Horse.

HEALING SOCKS

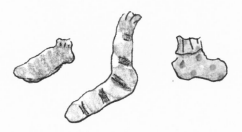

Turn to your single socks when you need a little comfort. With a bit of rice or a tennis ball or two, an odd sock can provide a massage or be a source of pain-relieving heat.

⊙ Fill a sock with rice, heat it in microwave for a minute or two, and place it on sore muscles (or use it to soothe a woman's labor pains). If you'd like to, you can add a scent like rosemary, peppermint, or sage. The rice-filled sock can also be frozen to reduce swelling at the site of an injury.

○ Put a tennis ball into a long sock and tie it. Holding the top of the sock, toss it behind you so that the ball lands on your back. With your back pressed against a wall, move so that the ball rolls against your back, massaging away aches and pains.

○ For the poor soul whose foot is in a cast, keep toes warm by pulling a large single sock over the cast.

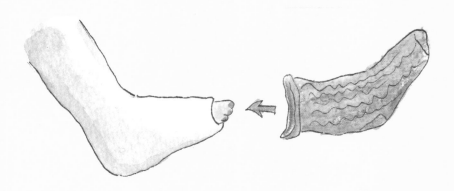

○ Tie a double knot in an odd sock. Lie on the floor and place the knotted sock under any area of your back or legs that is sore. Move gently on top of the sock, allowing the knot to press against areas that need to be massaged.

○ To loosen your neck and shoulders and alleviate tension, rest your neck on a sock filled with two tennis balls tied tightly into the toe of a sock. Arrange the sock so that one tennis ball is on either side of your spine.

⦿   If you need to apply a cold compress, put ice cubes in a ziplock baggie (or use a bag of frozen peas) and slide it into a sock for a more comfortable ice pack.

⦿   Make your own stress ball. Fill a single sock with beads, tie the end, and knead the ball with your hand. Say good-bye to tension.

other sock mysteries

In addition to ending up alone,
socks suffer from a wide range of ailments.
Here are just a few:

○ They change shape.

O They stretch to ridiculous lengths.

O Each one in a pair ends up an entirely different shape and size.

- They get hard.

- Even though a given pair of socks presumably has been worn to the same place at the same time, one often ends up pristine, whereas the other is covered with muck and weird purple stains.

The top gets completely stretched out.

SOCKS ON YOUR HANDS

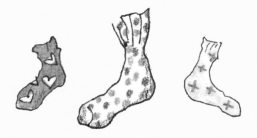

At first it might feel a little odd (your thumb will fight for its own space) but soon you'll come to love hands-on socks for all of the help they can provide. Put socks on your hands and . . .

. . . wash the dishes.

. . . wash your car.

. . . spray the socks with furniture polish
   and dust the furniture.

. . . hold dishes that are too hot for bare hands.

. . . polish silver.

. . . wash potatoes.

. . . wipe the slats of Venetian blinds.

. . . polish and shine your shoes.

. . . soap yourself up and scrub in the shower.

. . . clean the bathroom sink (using old toothpaste remnants or shaving cream splotches as soap).

. . . clean hard-to-reach places like the spindles on the backs of chairs or between railings on the stairs.

. . . change a hot light bulb.

HELPING SOCKS

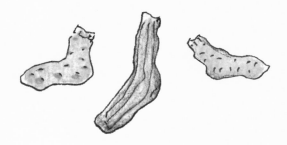

You may not be able to afford household help, but odd-sock help is available to everyone. These tips show you just how useful your socks can be. You'll never let them just hang around in a drawer again.

SOCKS THAT HELP CLEAN

◎   Use a rubber band to attach a sock (inside out, so the loops catch more dirt) to the end of a yard stick. Then push it under the refrigerator to clean. It can also be used to clean cobwebs in high corners.

◎   Cut off the toes and cut up the side of the sock for a sock rag.

◎   If your mop head is wearing out, pull a sock over it, secure it with a rubber band, and go after that floor!

sock matching game

Can you match these 10 very different single socks to make five wearable pairs?

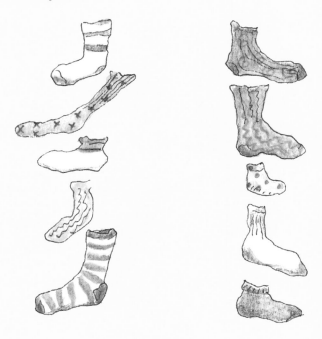

SOCKS THAT HELP WHEN FILLED

◎ Fill a sock with coffee, tie the end, and put it in the freezer to absorb odors.

◎ Collect leftover soap pieces in a sock, tie a knot, and use it as a loofah in the shower.

◎ Put moth balls in the toe of the sock, tie a knot, and tuck it among your wool sweaters when you store them in the off-season, or place them strategically in your closet. (If you don't like the smell of moth balls, you can use a combination of cedar shavings, cinnamon cloves, and dried lavender instead.)

○ Fill a sock with salt and use it to wipe your bathroom mirror. (This makes the mirror less likely to fog up.)

○ Fill a sock with kitty litter, tie a knot, and stuff it into a shoe that is damp or a little "fragrant." The kitty litter will absorb the odor and the moisture. (You can substitute herbs like cinnamon or balsam for the kitty litter if you'd prefer.)

OTHER KINDS OF HELPING SOCKS

If an object of value falls into the mud, put a sock over your hand to retrieve the item and keep your hands clean. (Bonus: You can use the sock to hold the item until you get home to wash it off.)

Use "ladder socks" to keep from marking walls in your house. If you will be leaning a ladder against a wall you'd like to protect, put socks on the ends of the ladder and secure them with rubber bands.

○ If someone in the house is sick, pull socks over phones and door knobs to keep the germs from spreading (and change them frequently).

○ Put a sock on the bottom of a jar of honey to keep the counter from getting sticky (or the bottom of an olive oil bottle to keep from leaving oily stains in the cupboard).

 If you need to carry something with an uncomfortable strap, like a computer bag, slide a sock (with the toe cut off) over the strap for extra cushioning.

◉ Use the stretchy top part of a sock as you would a large rubber band to hold rolled-up posters, large maps, or wrapping paper.

◉ When you are going to slide a heavy piece of furniture across a wood floor, put socks over the legs so that they won't leave scratch marks.

● If you are packing and moving, stuff odd socks into items that you don't want to be crushed, like shoes or hats.

● Wash a delicate undergarment inside a sock (tied at the top) to keep it safe.

● Use odd socks as additional socks in the wintertime when one pair isn't enough to keep your feet warm.

SAFETY SOCKS

Socks are safety conscious by nature, keeping feet warm, keeping feet from getting blisters, keeping feet from getting splinters if the feet wander onto the deck without shoes. Here are a few less conventional ways that socks can help keep you safe.

○ When transporting a sharp object, tuck it inside a few socks so that no one will get poked.

○ Before throwing broken glass into the trash, put it in a sock to protect the person who will take the trash out.

○ If a toy has a sharp piece, tuck it into a sock (or two) before putting it into a toy box.

○ Pull a sock over your hot cup of coffee or tea to protect your hands.

# the sock monster, as envisioned by various artists

by PICASSO

by RUBENS

by POLLOCK

SOCKS TO PROTECT

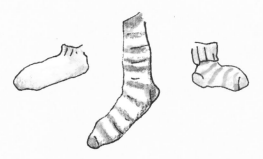

Forget about wrapping items in newspaper or bubble wrap.
Pull odd socks over things to protect them, such as . . .

. . . Christmas ornaments.

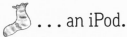 . . . an iPod.

 . . . a cell phone.

. . . fruit in a lunchbox.

 . . . a camera.

. . . yarn and knitting needles, to keep your project
    from unraveling.

. . . fragile items that are being packed
    for moving or storage.

. . . items in a picnic basket that might break, such as
    a jar of pickles, ketchup bottle, or a bottle of wine.

... case-less CDs or DVDs when you send them in the mail.

... buckles in the washing machine.

... fishing reels in a tackle box.

RETRO SOCKS

Like the polyester prints of the '70s that resurfaced a few years ago, these sock items may be back in style some day. You certainly wouldn't want your daughter to be the only one on the bus who didn't have a sock monkey, so hang on to these directions, just in case.

● Make hair curlers out of socks. Cut several socks into strips. Take a section of damp hair, tie the sock strip onto the section of hair and slide it down to within an inch of the end. Roll the hair as you would with a curler and tie at the scalp. The sock curlers are easy to sleep on and the curls will set overnight.

Cut the tube part of socks into loops and use them to make woven pot holders (remember Girl Scouts?). Anyone with a little time on her hands can stitch the pot holders together to make a one-of-a-kind rug.

○ Folks with the quaint, horse-shoe–shaped toilet seats can slip large socks onto each side to make a cozy seat cover. When the socks have served their purpose, they can be thrown away and easily replaced.

○ If your feet are often cold, try this tip from the olden days: sprinkle cayenne pepper into two odd socks and then slip your feet into them. Instant warmth!

○ Make a sock monkey.

ALL ABOUT SOCK MONKEYS

○ Sock monkeys date from the early 1900s when an Illinois-based company, Nelson Knitting Mills, inspired crafty folks with its signature Red Heel socks. The red heel provided the monkey's red lips, and the white toe gave the monkey a little cap. For instructions on how to make your very own sock monkey, visit www.supersockmonkey.com.

sockmatch.com

"Athletically inclined looking for sole mate"

Description: Age: 2 years old
Color: White
Height: 10"
Hair: None
Eyes: Ditto
Employment: Part-time; seasonal
Occupation: Protection of the foot
Marital Status: Separated
Living Situation: Living with other singles
Children: None
Interests: Dancing, hiking, jogging, or any activities associated with moving feet

Strong, comfortable sock that resists shrinking in search of same. Prefers sock with no added bulk that has kept its shape and softness after repeated washing. Color not a factor. Partial to the more exotic anklet, in linen or cashmere. Turn-ons: lace trim or bows.

FINGER KNITTING WITH
SOCKS

Finger knitting is surprisingly fun, in a Little-House-on-the-Prairie kind of way. You can easily finger knit a potholder if you don't have access to one of the mini looms used by the Girl Scouts. Here's how to do it:

○ Begin by cutting the "tube" parts of a few dozen socks into loops about an inch wide.

○ Thread a sock loop onto the four fingers of your left hand: wrap the loop around your index finger, twist once, then wrap around it your middle finger, twist once, and continue to your pinky.

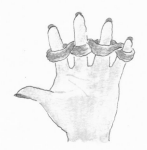

● Push the loops down on your fingers and repeat the process with a second sock piece so that one loop layer is on top of another.

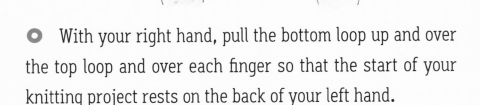

● With your right hand, pull the bottom loop up and over the top loop and over each finger so that the start of your knitting project rests on the back of your left hand.

● Repeat with the remaining loops.

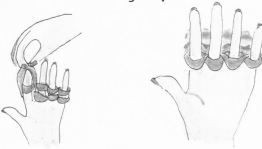

 # your sock drawer: before and after

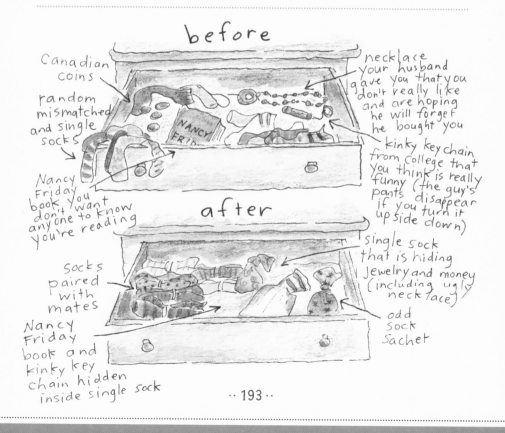

before

Canadian coins

random mismatched and single socks

Nancy Friday book you don't want anyone to know you're reading

necklace your husband gave you that you don't really like and are hoping he will forget he bought you

kinky key chain from college that you think is really funny (the guy's pants disappear if you turn it upside down)

after

Socks paired with mates

Nancy Friday book and kinky key chain hidden inside single sock

single sock that is hiding jewelry and money (including ugly necklace)

odd sock sachet

DAINTY SOCKS

These sock ideas are for those dainty gals who still appreciate the frugal touch.

 Make a sachet bag from an odd sock by filling it with dried lavender and tying it at the top. You can also use strong smelling soap in place of the lavender, and then use the soap for its intended purpose after the smell has faded.

○ Put lotion on your hands and feet at bedtime and then cover them with odd socks to keep the lotion where it belongs.

○   Put a cup of dried flowers into a sock, tie a knot, and put it in the dryer with damp laundry. Instant laundry refresher! To keep the scent strong, just squeeze the sock between loads.

○   Fill a sock with body powder, tie a tight knot, and then use it as a powder puff.

RANDOM SOCKS

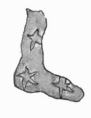

These sock tips may not fit into a standard category, but that doesn't make them any less useful. After all, if a burglar sneaks into your house in the dead of night, you'll be very glad you paid attention to the last odd sock use on page 200.

- Fill a sock with rice, tie the end, and use it to steady the front end of your rifle at a shooting range.

- Pull a sock over a block of wood to make a chalkboard eraser.

- Mail odd socks to Michael Jackson, under the assumption that he uses only one glove, so he likely uses only one sock, just to be consistent. In addition, he seems to like things that are odd.

- Put rocks in the toe end of a sock, tie a knot, and keep it next to your bed in case you need to use it to knock out an intruder.

sock drawers of famous people

Michael Jordan

Fred Flintstone

Your socks are missing! Clue:

Sherlock Holmes

SOCK CHART

Martha Stewart

Bindi Irwin

Albert Einstein

○   Make an indoor snowman out of an odd white sock. Fill the sock about two-thirds full with rice. Gently tie a piece of yarn around the sock to create a snowman belly. The upper part of the sock will be the snowman's head, with the ribbed top folded down like a hat. Decorate with buttons, beads, or anything else that says "snowman" to you.

basics for wearing mismatched socks

You wouldn't think there would be rules for wearing two different socks but there are . . . unspoken rules. If you follow them, you're a quirky free-spirit in your mismatched socks. If you don't, you may find yourself as a *Glamour* magazine fashion "don't," disguised by the black line across your eyes (but everyone will recognize you anyway).

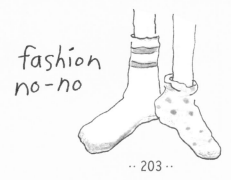

fashion no-no

○ The socks have to be very different in color. Wear one black sock and one navy blue sock and people just think you can't see very well.

○ The socks have to be the same length. No pairing an ankle sock with a tube sock. That has dressing-out-of-a-Dumpster written all over it.

○ The socks should both be a bit funky—striped, covered in dots, featuring Winnie the Pooh—something along that line. That way you're already on the path to cute and quirky.

About the author

needs glasses but pretends she doesn't ↘

← has hair that is too long for someone her age (but is trusting best friend Mary Brett to tell her kindly when it's time to get it cut)

talks too fast because she is easily excited

← has 2 holes in each ear because teenage daughter talked her into it

lives in → sweatshirts and pajama pants

← is afraid of new computer

always has a messy desk ↗

Cynthia L. Copeland
(call her "Cindy")

Best-selling, award-winning author Cynthia L. Copeland has written and illustrated more than 25 books for adults and children including *The Diaper Diaries* and *Really Important Stuff My Kids Have Taught Me.* She lives in rural New Hampshire with her family. Anya Lewis, the oldest of her three children, came up with the idea for this book during a rainy afternoon spent searching for pairs among hundreds of single socks.

ABOUT CIDER MILL PRESS

Good ideas ripen with time. From seed to harvest, Cider Mill Press strives to bring fine reading, information, and entertainment together between the covers of its creatively crafted books. Our Cider Mill bears fruit twice a year, publishing a new crop of titles each spring and fall.

CIDER MILL
PRESS

BOOK
PUBLISHERS

Where good books
are ready for press

Visit us on the web at:

www.cidermillpress.com

or write to us at:

12 Port Farm Road
Kennebunkport, Maine 04046